MW01141845

WEDDING GOWNS
GOWNS
& Other Bridal Apparel

WEDDING GOWNS
GOWNS
& Other Bridal Apparel

*Looking
Beautiful
on Your
Special Day*

JO PACKHAM

A Sterling/Chapelle Book
Sterling Publishing Co., Inc. New York

Jo Packham
Author

Cherie Hanson
Editor/Designer

Trice Boerens
Illustrator

Library of Congress Cataloging-in-Publication Data

Packham, Jo.
 Wedding gowns & other bridal apparel : looking beautiful on your
 special day / Jo Packham.
  p. cm.
 "A Sterling/Chapelle book."
 Includes index.
 ISBN 0-8069-0588-3
  1. Wedding costume—United States. I. Title. II. Title: Wedding
 gowns and other bridal apparel.
 GT1753.U6P32 1994
 392' .54—dc20   93-43684
                                                      CIP

10 9 8 7 6 5 4 3 2 1

A Sterling/Chapelle Book

Published by Sterling Publishing Company, Inc.
387 Park Avenue South, New York, N.Y. 10016
© 1994 by Chapelle Ltd.
Distributed in Canada by Sterling Publishing
$^{c}/_{o}$ Canadian Manda Group, P.O. Box 920, Station U
Toronto, Ontario, Canada M8Z 5P9
Distributed in Great Britain and Europe by Cassell PLC
Villiers House, 41/47 Strand, London WC2N 5JE, England
Distributed in Australia by Capricorn Link (Australia) Pty Ltd.
P.O. Box 6651, Baulkham Hills, Business Centre, NSW 2153, Australia
Manufactured in the United States of America
All rights reserved

Sterling ISBN 0-8069-0588-3

Contents

Introduction

A thing of beauty is a joy forever:
Its loveliness increases; it will never
Pass into nothingness; but still will keep
A bower quiet for us, and a sleep
Full of sweet dreams...

—*John Keats*

How many times have you closed your eyes and dreamed of the gown you will wear on your wedding day? The image is clear: a long dress with a cathedral train and hundreds of yards of lace; one of antique-ivory satin that resembles the one you saw in the old photographs from your grandmother's wedding; or one that is short, more contemporary, accented with a bouquet of gilded autumn leaves. Regardless of the fantasy, this is the time to make your "little girl's" dream come true.

Wedding Styles

The first decision that will affect which wedding dress you select is the style that you want your wedding to be. Will it be formal and very traditional? Will it follow an informal, contemporary theme, such as a Western barbecue? Or will it be something inbetween?

Whatever your decision, it should be reached by you and your fiancé together. It should fall within the limits of the budget you have set while at the same time reflecting both of your desires and dreams. Following, you will find a brief description as well as a very condensed chart to give you an overall picture of what each style traditionally represents.

Very Formal/Formal

Steeped in tradition and laced with all of the pageantry and finery the occasion has to offer is the very formal/formal wedding. The ceremony is eloquent and religious, the wedding party is extensive, the gowns are grand, the men are dressed in tails, and a limousine delivers you and your father to the church and drives you and the groom to the reception that follows—which is always truly an event to remember. It is large and lavish, with a sit-down dinner, music for dancing, and decorations to admire. The flowers are extraordinary and the wedding cake is a work of art. The grand finale of such a fine event is the limousine driving off with the groom and you, his beloved.

Semi-Formal

Most very formal/formal wedding procedures apply to the somewhat smaller, semiformal wedding events; they are simply done on a less lavish scale.

You will have fewer guests, the ceremony may or may not be of a religious nature, the wedding party consists of one to three attendants with the same number of groomsmen, and the reception can be very beautiful but less ostentatious.

Informal

An informal wedding event is often more intimate and can be held anywhere from a small chapel to your home. Guests are welcomed and directed by a member of the wedding party who is familiar with almost everyone invited. You are dressed in a lovely dress and the groom is sporting a business suit; the two of you will mingle with the guests before the ceremony. The reception for the informal wedding usually does not include more than 50 guests, an attendant for both you and the groom, and a small, symbolic wedding cake.

Traditional

Traditional wedding events usually have the ceremony performed in a church or temple by a clergy member with a reception to follow at a grand hotel or country club. There are many variations on the traditional wedding events, depending upon the restrictions placed by religion or local custom.

Nontraditional

Some couples think that the taking of vows in a church or hotel with any type of tradition attached is entirely too mainstream for their wants or needs. They prefer an event that is associated with what they love to do together the most; those who love to ski can be married in designer ski wear on the slopes, scubadivers can be clad in the latest-style wetsuit while taking their vows underwater, or you could be wed in true cowboy jeans on horseback with a barbecue to follow. Whatever you want is exactly the way the nontraditional wedding attire and festivities should be planned and executed.

If you prefer a nontraditional wedding and reception, but do not care to go to the extremes of being married underwater and steaming clams on the beach, then an alternative to consider is a wedding which falls somewhere in the middle. You might consider being married in a hunting lodge in the middle of the redwoods, dressed in a long, floral dress with flowers in your hair; or you may choose a historical site, with you, the groom, and your guests clad in period costumes. Home garden weddings and resort weddings are also considered nontraditional, but they have become so popular in today's society that young brides think they are having "a most traditional garden wedding."

Whichever you choose, anything from the very most formal to the very most contemporary, the choice should be one that you and the groom decide on together, that reflects your lifestyle, and that fits nicely into your budget. Do not worry too much whether the attire you have chosen conforms with the "rules" for the size and location of your wedding. If both of you are comfortable with your choice, then it is acceptable.

	Very Formal	Formal	Semi-Formal	Informal
Style	Traditional, expensive, elaborate	More relaxed, most popular	Between formal and informal	Whatever you desire
Invitations/Announcements	Engraved on heavy, white or ivory paper; card folded; two envelopes; enclosures	Engraved or printed on heavy white or ivory paper; single or folded card-one or two envelopes; enclosures	Printed on any color paper, additions such as photographs; one envelope	Printed, hand-written on any color paper or style that is appropriate is acceptable
Ceremony	Church, synagogue, temple, ballroom	Church, synagogue, temple, ballroom, home, country club	Anywhere that is appropriate	Anywhere desired
Reception	Large, lavish dinner and music	Dinner and music	Usually includes meal, maybe music	Small and simple
Food/Beverages	Champagne, wine or liquor and assorted beverages	Champagne or punch, other drinks optional	Champagne for toasts, other drinks optional	Champagne for toasts, tea, coffee, other drinks optional
	Sit-down or large buffet, bridal party and guests have tables	Buffet, bridal party may have tables	Stand-up buffet	Snacks or cake

	Very Formal	Formal	Semi-Formal	Informal
Decorations/Accessories	Elaborate flowers for church and reception. Canopy, pew ribbons, aisle carpet, limousines, groom's cake, engraved napkins	Flowers for church, same accessories as Very Formal Limousines and other items optional	Flowers for altar, same decorations for reception	Whatever you desire
Music	Organ at church, choir optional, dancing at reception	Organ at church, soloist optional, dancing optional	Organ at church	Usually no music
Guest List	Over 200 guests	75 - 200 guests	Under 100 guests	Not more than 50 guests
Bride	Elegant, long dress, long sleeves/ gloves, long train, veil	Long dress, any sleeve length, veil, shorter train	Morning wedding-knee length Evening-floor length, veil/hat/ wreath	Dress or suit or whatever you desire
Males	Cutaway, long jacket or stroller for day; tailcoat for night	Cutaway, stroller or tuxedo for day; tuxedo for night	Stroller, tuxedo dinner jacket for day; tuxedo, dinner jacket suit or blazer for evening	Business suit, blazer
Females	6 - 8 attendants, long dress	2 - 6 attendants, long dress	1 - 3 attendants, dress based on length, style of bride's	1 attendant, dress or suit or casual

History of the Gown

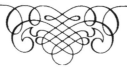

*I*n days long past, the traditional bridal gown was believed to have mystical value, which often prompted family and friends to try to seize a piece of enchanted lace or ribbon from the bride's dress for their own good-luck charm. Today, however, most women who choose a "traditional" wedding gown are fulfilling the memories of childhood dreams and the very special feelings of wearing a dress that is long and white and covered with beads and lace. Such a dream was first introduced by Empress Eugenie, a leader in the fashion world during her era. She wore a white gown at her wedding to Napoleon III, who ruled France from 1853 to 1871. Victorian brides who were from privileged backgrounds followed the Empress's example to show their sense of high fashion and to indicate their financial ability by being able to wear a dress for one day only.

In early Saxon days and through the 18th century, the poorer bride was dressed for her wedding day in a long, plain white robe. This was a public statement that she brought nothing with her to the marriage and therefore her husband was not responsible for her or her family's debts. Brides of higher social and financial standing simply wore their Sunday-best or the favorite fashion and color of the times. Chinese brides traditionally selected gowns of red, which was symbolic of celebration, and Icelandic brides chose black velvet embroidered with silver and gold. Colors worn by brides were often chosen for their symbolism as well as personal preference. Blue meant constancy, green meant youth, yellow signified jealousy and therefore was never, ever worn. Brides of ancient Israel wore a blue ribbon on the shoulder of their robes to symbolize purity, fidelity and love, but over the years the blue ribbon was abandoned and, in many cultures, the white wedding gown has come to symbolize purity and the utmost fidelity.

Today, however, there are no longer guidelines imposed by the style of wedding you have selected that dictate how your dress should look, what the fabric should be, or how long your veil and gown must be.

Blessed are those who can please themselves.

—South African Proverb

Wedding Gowns of Today

L isted below are traditional guidelines to
help you understand what was customarily
appropriate for wedding gowns and attire. What
is most important today, however, is that after
reviewing the list you select the gown that you
want and in which you feel most comfortable.

Traditional Style Guidelines

Season, location, and religious or local customs often dictate the fabrics you will select for
your wedding gown. If season and location are
the prime concern, in fall and winter you might
choose crepe, taffeta, satin, moiré, brocade,
velvet, or peau de soie. In the spring and summer months you will feel more comfortable in
silk, chiffon, lace, linen, piqué, eyelet, light-
weight satin, cotton, or chintz. If ethnic custom
is most important to you, you may choose
whatever is traditional—an Indian sari, a Japanese kimono, or a traditional red Chinese
wedding dress, for example.

Nontraditional Style Guidelines

Here you are free to do whatever you choose
as long as it is agreeable to both you and the
groom, in keeping with the theme of the festivities, and done in good taste. You may choose
anything from cowboy boots and a western shirt
to an antique-lace gown with brocade satin
shoes.

Very Formal Wedding Attire Guidelines

Gowns are usually floor-length in formal satin,
lace, or peau de soie with cathedral or chapel-
length trains. Veils are full-length, and headpieces are decorated with lace, beading, or
flowers. Bouquets are often large and elaborate.
Shoes can be either unadorned satin dyed to
match your gown or elaborately decorated with
beads and lace. Long gloves are often worn to
complement short-sleeved or sleeveless gowns.
Jewelry is optional but, if worn, should be
classically simple and of heirloom quality, such
as a single pendant or a string of pearls.

Formal Wedding Attire Guidelines

Gowns are a little less elaborate; they are
floor-length with chapel-length or sweeping
trains. A fingertip-length veil, decorated head

piece or hat should be worn. With short sleeves, if gloves are worn, they should be white kid, lace, or matching fabric. Bouquets are often small but can range from the very simple to the very ornate. Shoes and other accessories follow those of the very formal style.

Semi-Formal Wedding Attire Guidelines

A simple, floor-length gown, usually without a train, or an elaborate afternoon-style dress is most often worn. Veils are short with street-length dresses, longer with floor-length, or any style of hair piece is appropriate. Bouquets and other accessories are understated and simple.

Informal Wedding Attire Guidelines

Dresses are street-length and appropriate to the season and style of the festivities and are usually worn without a veil. Bouquets or corsages are often carried or worn, and all other accessories are more of an everyday nature.

After deciding the style of the wedding festivities, you and your fiancé will need to come to an agreement on how you both will be attired in relation to the wedding style you have selected and the budget you have arrived upon for such attire. Your wardrobe will depend somewhat on how the groom pictures himself dressed and how important the wedding attire is in the overall picture of the wedding festivities. Remember that you not only need to buy your dress, but must also budget money for a veil and other accessories. Hosiery, shoes, jewelry, and lingerie can total hundreds of dollars if you are not careful and do not plan ahead. After you have thoroughly discussed the attire for the day and have come to a general understanding, you will want to begin to get serious about your gown and your accessories. You must feel like everything is just the way you have always wanted it to be in order for you to feel as beautiful as your family and friends will think you are.

You will want everything to be perfect—and perfection comes with careful planning, attention to details, and allowing adequate time to complete every phase of the process. Begin actively shopping for your gown at least six months prior to the wedding date, or nine months if you have scheduled a wedding portrait to be taken several weeks before the wedding or if your dress is a special order from a prominent designer. Many design houses require a minimum of six months to order a gown from the manufacturer or a local renowned designer. If your dress has to be made or special-ordered, you will want to make certain you have allowed ample time for ordering, altering, or returning the gown or accessories should there be problems. There are so many people involved in the chain of events associated with a wedding gown that anything could go wrong with any one of them.

Married in white, you have chosen all right;
Married in grey, you will go far away;
Married in black, you will wish yourself back;
Married in red, you wish yourself dead;
Married in green, ashamed to be seen;
Married in blue, he will always be true;
Married in pearl, you will live in a whirl;
Married in yellow, ashamed of your fellow;
Married in brown, you will live out of town.
Married in pink, your fortune will sink.

—Anonymous Victorian Verse

How and where should you begin? Start by familiarizing yourself with the terms used in association with wedding gowns.

Lace

Alençon—a handmade, needlepoint lace with designs on sheer net outlined with cord. It originated in Alençon, France. It is very delicate.

Brussels Lace—a light and delicate lace with subtle patterns that is very beautiful and very expensive.

Chantilly—a fine, handmade mesh with scroll and floral designs, often with scalloped edges outlined with silk threads. It originated in Chantilly, France.

Cluny Lace—a lace made of fine linen thread, usually in open designs.

Schiffli—an expensive, machine-made lace, usually with fine, delicate floral embroidery.

Venice—a heavy, raised cotton or linen needlepoint lace with floral sprays, foliage, or geometrical designs, which was first made in Venice.

Fabrics

Batiste—a soft, delicate summer fabric made of cotton or a cotton-linen blend; the texture is fine and sheer.

Brocade—a heavy fabric with interwoven raised designs.

Charmeuse—a lightweight, smooth, semi-lustrous silk or synthetic fabric.

Chiffon—a fabric with a simple weave—often of silk or rayon—with a soft or stiff finish that is delicately sheer.

Chintz—a cotton fabric with a glazed finish.

Cotton—a popular natural fiber known for its reasonable cost and its versatility in texture, weight, and construction.

Crepe—a soft, fluid, summer fabric of silk, cotton, polyester, or rayon. The texture is finely crinkled or ridged.

Crepe de Chine—a soft, light, thin fabric of silk, rayon, or polyester. Used mostly for informal gowns in fall or winter.

Crinoline—an underskirt foundation used to extend the skirt of the wedding gown.

English Net—a fine, sheer cotton netting; a traditional but expensive fabric used in wedding gowns.

Eyelet—a silk, cotton, or cotton-polyester open-weave embroidery used mostly for decoration. It has small, round, holes finished at the edges with lace and/or embroidery.

Faille—a heavier, crisp, flat-ribbed fabric of silk or rayon that is used mostly for fall and winter weddings.

Georgette—a silk or synthetic crepe with a dull texture.

Illusion—a silk tulle or nylon material from which most veils are made.

Jersey—a soft, fluid material made of wool, silk, or rayon which usually has a satin or matte finish.

Lace—any open-weave fabric used for trim or the entire piece of clothing; see specific kinds of lace on page 21.

Linen—made from flax, this fiber has been used for clothing since the dawn of civilization. It is beautiful, durable and elegant, with a natural luster and is used for spring and summer weddings.

Moiré—a silk taffeta that, when illuminated, glistens like water.

Net—an open-weave mesh fabric often used in veils.

Nylon—a man-made fiber which is produced in a wide variety of fabric textures, from smooth to crisp to soft and bulky. It can be heat-set to hold pleats and embossed designs.

Organdy—a very fine, sheer fabric, usually cotton, with a stiff finish.

Organza—a sheer, crisply textured fabric which is almost transparent. It may be embroidered with patterns of flowers having rolled edges that are often lightly colored; it is then called embroidered organza.

Peau de Soie—winter dress material made of blended fabrics that has a light, silky texture and a dull, satin like finish.

Piqué—a ribbed fabric known for its distinct texture and made of cotton, rayon, or silk.

Point d'Esprit—a net or tulle with dots woven into the pattern.

Rayon—a man-made fiber that can resemble many natural fibers. It drapes well and has a good affinity for dyes.

Satin—a silk or synthetic material with a smooth, usually shiny, unbroken surface.

Silk—a beautiful, luxurious natural fabric available in a variety of weaves and weights which holds brilliant color. Silk chiffon is sheer and drapes well; silk brocade is stiff and elegant.

Shantung—a rough-textured plain-weave silk or man-made fiber.

Silk-Faced Satin—a full-bodied satin with an antique sheen.

Slipper Satin—a lustrous, light, soft, more closely woven satin fabric made primarily of acetate.

Taffeta—a crisp, smooth, glossy fabric with a small crosswise web.

Tulle—a fine, sheer net fabric of cotton, nylon, rayon or silk.

Velvet—a cold-weather fabric made of silk, cotton, or a silk-cotton blend. The fiber is a thick, soft pile with a matte finish.

Voile—a light, open-weave fabric of wool, silk, cotton, or cotton-polyester blend that is used for informal dress styles.

I am not fully dressed until I adorn myself with a smile of joy.

—*Author Unknown*

Silhouettes

A-Line—tapered or tight-fitting bodice, with a close-fitting waist that slowly tapers to a flared hem.

Antebellum—dress with a tight-fitting bodice, with a natural waistline that dips two inches to a point in the center front.

Asymmetrical—fabric falls to one side from the natural waistline.

Ballgown—an off-the-shoulder bodice accented by a natural waistline with a lavish, full skirt.

Blouson—drooping fullness in the fabric from the bodice to the waist, gathered at or below the waist.

Bustle Back—a gown with an exaggerated fullness in the rear of the skirt, built with a pad or frame. This is often done with a bridal train for easier movement at the reception.

Drop Waist—the bodice may be loose, tapered, or tightly fitted, with the waistline of the dress dropping several inches below the natural waist.

Empire—small, scooped bodice gathering at a high waist with a slim yet full skirt. (A raised waist is a waistline that is about one inch above the natural waistline— which may or may not be an empire waist.)

Princess—slim-fitting bodice and skirt with vertical seams flowing from the shoulder to the hem of the skirt; accentuates the waist but does not hug the body.

Sheath—narrow, body-hugging style without a waist.

Ah, great it is to believe the dream
As we stand in youth by the starry stream;
But a greater thing is to fight life through,
And say at the end, "The dream is true!"

—Edwin Markham

Skirts

Belle—a circular cut that is full and usually a longer length.

Bouffant—a very full, puffed-out skirt.

Dirndl—a gathered skirt, not especially full, with a tight waistband.

Full—is gathered, but less full than the bouffant style.

Hoop—the underskirt is stiffened with circular hoops made of boning.

Peplum—a short flounce or overskirt that is attached at the waistline.

Skirt with Shirred Waist—fabric is gathered to make a horizontal panel at the waistline of the skirt.

Tiered—a skirt that has a series of layered panels falling in graduated lengths.

Trumpet—tapers close to the legs, then flares at or below the knee.

Belle

Full

Dirndl

Peplum

Necklines

High—collar just brushing the chin.

Sabrina—a high, slightly curved neck.

Queen Elizabeth—the high collar stands up in the back and comes to a closed V in the front.

Jewel—fabric encircles the natural neckline.

Square—neckline is shaped like half of a square in the front and may be the same in the back or high and straight.

Sweetheart—the front neckline is shaped like the top half of a heart with the back being higher and straight across from shoulder to shoulder.

Off-the-Shoulder—the neckline falls below the shoulders and hovers above the bustline (but the dress has sleeves).

Boat (or Bateau or Scoop)—the neckline gently follows the curve of the collarbone almost to the tip of the shoulders in the front and the same in the back.

Queen Anne—the neckline rises high at the nape (back) of the neck, then sculpts low in the front either in a sweetheart shape or to outline a bare yoke.

Collars

Bertha—a cape of fabric or lace that is attached to the neckline for a shawl effect.

Wedding Band—an upright collar which encircles the base of the neck and is often made of lace.

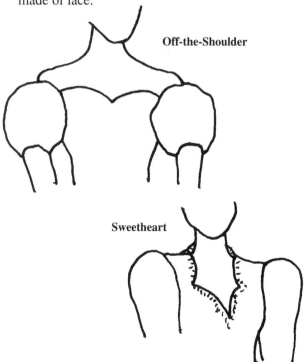

Off-the-Shoulder

Sweetheart

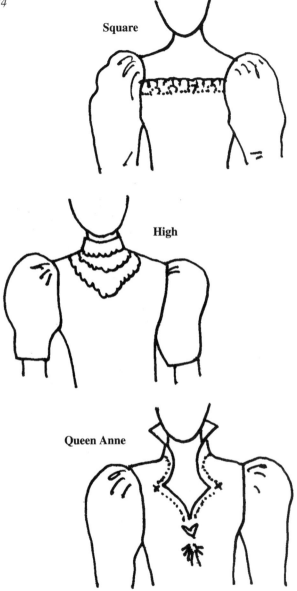

Square

High

Queen Anne

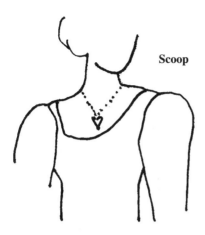

Scoop

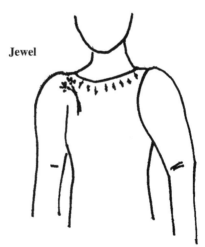

Jewel

Sleeves

Bishop—fuller in the lower forearm, then gathered at the wrist into a wide cuff.

Cap—a small sleeve just covering the top of the arm.

Capelet—falls several inches below the elbow in a soft flare.

Dolman—a sleeve which extends from the armhole so large that it creates a cape-like effect. It is often fitted at the wrist.

Fitted—a narrow long sleeve.

Gibson—is full at the shoulder and fitted at the wrist.

Leg-of-Mutton (or Gigot)—a sleeve which is wide and rounded at the shoulder, tapering to a snug fit on the lower arm.

Melon—a sleeve which is extravagantly rounded from the shoulder to the elbow.

Peek-a-Boo—is a sheer, puffed sleeve that has a different fabric showing through underneath.

Poet—the style is pleated at the shoulder and is very full from shoulder to cuff.

Pointed—a long, fitted sleeve that falls into a point below the wrist and over the top of the hand.

Puff—a short sleeve gathered into a gentler rounded shape usually above the elbow.

Three-Quarter—a sleeve which ends between the elbow and the wrist.

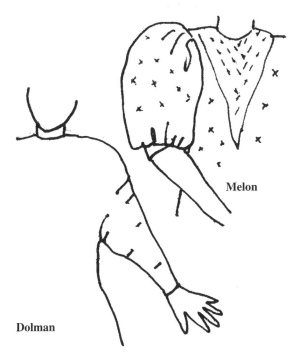

Melon

Dolman

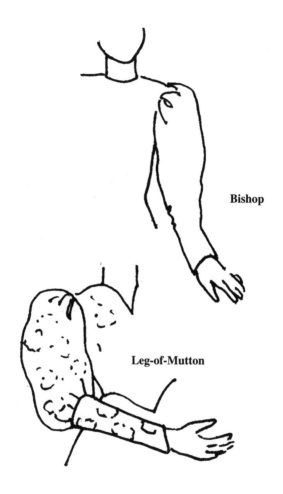

Bishop

Leg-of-Mutton

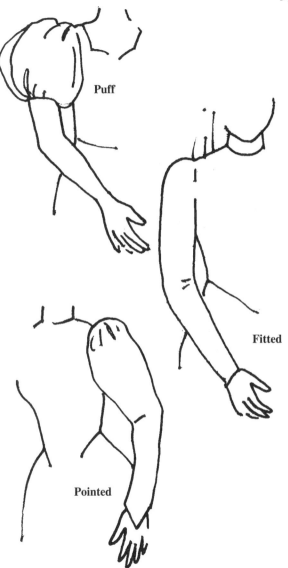

Puff

Fitted

Pointed

Dress Lengths

Street—hem just covering the knees.

Intermission—hem slightly below the knee in front and falling to ankle length in back.

Ballet—hem reaching to the center of the calf or slightly below.

Tea—a gown that falls several inches above the ankles.

Floor—hem fully skimming the floor.

Trains

Sweep or Brush—the shortest train, barely touching the floor.

Court—a train which is one foot longer than the sweep train.

Chapel—a train which extends about $1\frac{1}{3}$ yards from the waist. This is the most popular train of young brides of today.

Cathedral—a train which cascades $2\frac{1}{2}$ yards from the waist. This is the train used in very formal wedding ceremonies.

Royal—flowing more than 3 yards from the waist. This is the longest train.

Caplet Train—flows from the back of the shoulders.

Watteau—the train falls from the back yoke of the dress.

Detachable Train—a train that is joined to the gown at the waistline with hooks and eyes, and can be removed for the reception.

In every man's heart there is a secret nerve that answers to the vibrations of beauty.

—Christopher Morley

Wedding Gown Selection Tips

*B*efore selecting your wedding gown, begin looking at the dozens of designs in bridal fashion magazines and visit several bridal salons. You will want to browse through the stock they have on hand and ask to see their special-order catalogs. Ask your fiancé, mother, or one special friend to come along, not only to share your excitement but to offer support. Another person can help you keep your perspective and offer genuinely useful suggestions or advice. You want someone who will have an objective opinion, help you to stay within your budget, and pay attention to the details you might overlook. However, one companion is enough. Because selecting your wedding gown is fraught with emotion, you do not need "too much help" or conflicting opinions from too many people.

When looking for a bridal shop, you may wish to use the following sources:

Bridal Magazines—The major bridal magazines have pages and pages of advertisements from reputable wedding-apparel manufacturers, usually with names and addresses of stores that carry their lines.

Friends—Ask family and friends for their recommendations. This is especially helpful if they have been closely associated with someone who has recently been married.

Bridal Consultant or Wedding Coordinator—A consultant or coordinator is so actively involved in wedding planning and arrangements that he or she is usually informed as to which salons are reputable.

The Better Business Bureau—Check to make certain that the shops you are considering do not have a record of complaints. Any complaint, even if it is resolved, should send up a red flag.

Choose only reputable salons in which to do your shopping, and use discretion in giving the salesperson your name, phone number, and wedding date. It is not uncommon for sales-people to align themselves with photographers, caterers, florists, and others, giving them the names of newly engaged couples in return for receiving a commission if the bride elects to use their services. Receiving such unsolicited calls can be very time-consuming and annoying, especially if you have already made your choices for these services. If you have not, you may wish to ask the salesperson for any referrals she might have.

Points to remember when selecting a reputable bridal salon are:

1. Many bridal salons remove the tags from their wedding gowns, especially sample gowns in stock for the purpose of special ordering, to prevent you from knowing who designed and manufactured the gown. They hope to keep you from price comparing at another salon or from ordering the gown directly from the manufacturer on your own.

2. Beware of the salesperson who begins by showing you the most expensive dresses in stock and then "gushes" and makes a fuss over every gown that you try on, telling you that this is truly the perfect dress for such a special day. Most salespeople work on commission, so you must be critical of what is said and make certain they show you only gowns that are in your budget.

3. Be sure to ask for all fees for alterations, additions and/or subtractions from your gown. Many salons make a full mark-up on the sale of the gown and then, charge unreasonably high additional prices to have it altered, to have beads added, or to have lace removed.

4. Compare the prices of the salon's accessories to those in a regular department store. Due to your emotional state and the time restraints to get everything accomplished, brides often buy without price comparisons. One-stop shopping is so much easier and the accessories match the gown perfectly! For this reason, the salon can charge unreasonably high prices for accessories and you may not even be aware of what you are gladly paying them.

5. Be careful of "sales" and "discounts." Many shops mark their dresses and accessories up so that they can mark them down to make you feel that you are getting a good deal and to force you into making a quick decision. Beware of pressure to "buy now or be unable to take advantage of the sale or discounted price"!

6. Be wary of salons which say they have an "exclusive" arrangement with the designer and that you will be unable to find the

gown and/or matching accessories anywhere else in town. In some limited situa-
tions this may be true, but you will need to
make certain and not let this tactic prevent
you from shopping elsewhere.

If you are not planning on a traditional wedding gown, you may still find it helpful to look
through fashion magazines for the latest styles.
Plan on visiting an exclusive boutique or the
designer department at your local high-end
department store. If you want something very
out of the ordinary and do not live in San
Francisco or New York, look for your dream
dress while on vacation; resort areas often have
unique and hand-designed fashion clothing and/
or accessories.

Allow several days to shop and try on dresses.
If you try to do it all in one day, it is tiring,
confusing, and may cause you to make a decision that you will regret later. If you are going to
a bridal salon or the bridal department of a large
department store, make an appointment so that
you are guaranteed the attention that such an
important decision requires. This decision is
certainly the most emotional one you will ever
make in regard to something to wear!

You may want to begin by taking with you a picture or a drawing of the dress you have in mind. If you find a picture of a dress in a wedding magazine that interests you, *save the entire magazine* to show the salesperson in the salon. The information he or she will need to order the exact gown you have selected is often not on the page with the picture but someplace else in the magazine. Remember, however, to be open-minded; try as they might, the shop may not be able to find the dress you have chosen. Or, you may be surprised to find that the shop has the "perfect" dress and it is completely different than the one you had imagined!

Be very careful; it is so easy to get swept up in the moment when you see yourself in a fabulous gown. Ultimately, you need to choose a gown that is within your budget and that is in keeping with the style of your wedding. It may be less confusing in the end if you only try on gowns that are within your budget. Do not let the clerk talk you into something you do not want or cannot afford.

Be certain to ask the clerk about every detail of the dress you are ordering or trying on. Is it one-of-a-kind or mass-produced? What is the designer's name? What is the fabric? Knowledge of fabrics is important because silk, for example, is very fragile and difficult to care for. Rayon has sizing that is removed with the first cleaning, while cotton, nylon and other fabrics are easier to wear and to preserve. Check the manufacturer's instructions for the cleaning and care of the gown. If they are not on the dress, be sure you ask the salesperson and receive the instructions in writing. If you are told to care for the dress or accessories in a specific manner by the employee of the salon and it causes the dress to be ruined, you will have some recourse when you have written proof of the instructions given.

Selecting the Right Gown for You

When selecting a gown, first check with the ceremony officiant or coordinator to make certain there are no religious restrictions on the gown you must wear. Certain faiths require a particular neck height or some style of sleeve. Choose a dress that is a style which is appropriate for the season and that you feel comfortable in, as well as one that looks attractive on you and is flattering to your figure. Watch how it moves when you walk and how it looks from the back (remember that most of your guests will see more of you from the back than any other way). Know what is best suited for your body type.

These general guidelines may be helpful in selecting a dress that is best for your figure type:

If You Are Short and Petite (5' 4" and under), look for salons which carry petite-sized dresses. To create an illusion of height, you will want a dress with seams or lace appliqués which run up and down lengthwise. You may want to consider a high neckline, A-line, empire, or princess silhouettes, small collars and cuffs, short sleeves or sleeveless with long gloves, or dresses that are trim at the neckline and shoulders to draw the eye upward. You should stay away from a belt, unless it is a very narrow one. Also, consider a chapel train with a floor-length veil. Try to avoid frills and excessive detailing.

If You Are Tall and Slender (5' 9" plus), you will want to look for dresses with trims that wrap completely around the gown and veil, wide midriffs and sashes, large collars, big cuffs, raglan or butterfly sleeves, flared or tiered skirts and low necklines.

If You Are Thin, you can choose fabrics that are softly draping or heavier and have texture or a bold pattern. They may have a sheen, nap, or horizontal ribbing, such as satins, velvets, and brocades. Choose a dress with a full, gathered,

or dirndl skirt with lots of ornamentation.
Consider long, full sleeves, a bloused-bodice
top, a cropped jacket, a sash in a contrasting
color, or a wide sculpted collar.

If You Are a Stick Figure (I want to be just like
you!) with little shape, you will need to create
one. Ornamentation should appear on both upper
and lower body to provide balance in both areas.
Gowns with oversized shoulders, a jewel or
bateau neckline and elaborately detailed sleeves
are best. You also want a large skirt with horizontal styling made in a fabric that will hold its
shape. Try to avoid high-waisted dresses or slim
silhouettes with vertical styling which will make
you look still taller and thinner.

If You Are Pear-Shaped, which is narrow above
the waist and heavy below, you will want to
choose a gown with a long, textured bodice and
abundant trim. This creates the illusion of a
fuller upper body, while drawing the eyes to that
area. Full sleeves that extend the shoulder also
help. The skirt should accentuate the waist and
be simple with controlled fullness. Stay away
from slim, sheath silhouettes; very full skirts;
heavy ornamentation in the hip area; and high
necklines which make the shoulder look nar-
rower.

If You Have an Hour-Glass Shape, with your bust and hip measurements being equal and your waist about ten inches smaller than either, you will want to make the most of your waist by balancing your proportions in simple classic lines. Off-the-shoulder sleeves and plunging necklines are fine. You do not want too much detail on the bodice or skirt; they have a tendency to make you look too heavy.

If You Are Full-Figured, consider a princess silhouette featuring vertical panels with no waist seam or the straight, sleek lines of a chemise. Avoid heavy materials, clinging materials, bold patterns, contrasting colors, or figure-hugging styles, such as the sheath or trumpet skirt. You might want to consider choosing a floating material that will help to hide the pounds. To minimize hips, a dropped-V waist will be most flattering. Leg-of-mutton sleeves, which are full and then taper downward, flatter full arms. Intricate embroidery near the neckline draws attention to your facial features as will a V or shallow U neckline. Vertical beading on the center, rather than the sides, of the gown elongates the body. Consider carefully before choosing abundant ruffles, flounces, or layers of lace that may add inches to your proportions.

If You Have a Thick Midriff and Waist, choose the slimming effect of a lifted waistline and A-line skirt. Avoid tight waists, belts and cummerbunds, and shaped midriffs in contrasting colors.

If You Have a Very Slender Midriff and Waist (Realize how lucky you are!), accentuate your features with a dress featuring a well-defined midriff, a gathered or pleated skirt, and a natural or sashed waistline.

If You Have Narrow Shoulders, drape them with cape collars or capelets. Accentuate them with sleeves that gather at the top, necklines that are bare or widely curved, and shoulder pads built into the dress.

If You Have Broad Shoulders, look for dresses with smooth, set-in sleeves, low V necklines or high, covered necks. Avoid puffed or leg-of-mutton sleeves, bare necklines, broad collars, haltered tops and shoulder pads.

If You Are Big-Busted, you may wish to stay with elongated bodices and necklines that are V- or U-shaped or high with a keyhole yoke. Avoid cinched waists, empire styles that come up high under the bust, and clingy fabrics that accentuate your fullness. Choose instead full, billowing skirts with lots of ornamentation, which will create a curvier lower body. Keep sleeves simple with a natural shoulder line, and avoid adornments on the bodice.

If You Have Wide Hips, choose an A-line or gently flared half circle of a skirt, and balance yourself top and bottom by selecting a broad collar or portrait neckline and puffed sleeves.

It would be wise for you to shop for several days, trying gowns on in a few different stores. When you first begin the ritual of seeing and trying on gowns, the salesperson will inquire as to the budget you have for your gown. It is a good idea to reveal an amount that is slightly lower—maybe as much as 25%—than you have actually allocated for your dress and accessories. The majority of salespeople will try to influence you to buy up. If you have $1,000 budgeted, tell the salesperson $750. Make anywhere from one to three selections, and ask the salespeople to hold the gowns for up to a week while you think about them. Note which points about the gowns that you like and do not like. List which and what style of accessories should accompany the dresses you have selected. If the clerk will allow you to do so, have the person with you take pictures of you in the gowns you have selected. You can have the pictures developed quickly and study them at home at your leisure.

After a week has passed, style your hair the way you think you will be wearing it the day of the wedding, wear appropriate lingerie, wear a pair of shoes the height you will be wearing, select any accessories you have that you are certain will be included, and return to try the dresses on again. It is amazing how many times a bride forgets something that is very important in regard to the attire she will be wearing. You may also remember the dress differently than it really is or, when you return, you may not have remembered several of the important details of the gown that you thought at the time were essential.

The price of your gown will be based on the originality of the design or the designer's name that is attached, the intricacy of the dress style, the type of material, the amount of handwork required to attach the details, and the number of alterations needed to the original design. Custom gowns are the most expensive. The least expensive are those you buy off the rack at a department store, purchase secondhand, rent from a bridal salon, make yourself, or that you borrow. To ensure that the gown is worth the price being paid, make certain to examine it carefully. What type of material and lace are being used? How nicely are the buttons, zippers, and seams put together? Is the trim glued on, sewn by machine or hand stitched? Is it an original or mass-produced?

When choosing a dress that needs to be special-ordered, you will probably have to have alterations made. The salesperson can take your exact measurements for reference, using a vinyl tape measure to assure accuracy, and pin the sample gown so that it is closest to your size. He or she will then order the estimated size from the manufacturer. Do not order a size smaller than you actually are on the day of the fitting because you are certain you will lose weight before your wedding day! It is much easier to take a dress in than it is to let it out, and the whole point of having the dress special-ordered is so that you will have a perfect fit. When the dress finally arrives at the shop, you will then go in for your first fitting. If you are buying a dress off of the rack, chances are it will also need to be altered in one or two places so that it fits you perfectly and comfortably. You may also wish to make additions to or deletions from the dress—more pearls, less lace or a shorter hem.

When determining if you have a proper fit, consider the following points:

Neck—No style should be so loose that it gaps at the neckline. A rounded neckline should settle at the hollow base of your throat; a high neckline should be taut but comfortable.

Bust—The bodice of the gown should lay smoothly across your bosom. If it is a fitted style, it should be snug but not so tight it begins to flatten. Darts should be in line with the fullest part of your bosom. Side seams should extend from the armhole to the hem in a straight line.

Sleeve—If your sleeve style is supposed to fit tightly, there is no way around the fact that arm movements will be somewhat restricted. The cuff should rest at your wrist bone, with any lace or trim extending over your upper hand. Shoulder seams should lie on top of the shoulder and be invisible at the front of the dress.

Waist—If there are bubbles or wrinkles, the dress is too long-waisted and should be altered. Make certain that it is not too tight; the day will be a long one and you will want to be comfortable.

Length—Your gown should be 1½ to 2 inches off the floor when you are wearing your wedding shoes. If you want it to touch the floor, make certain that the wedding ceremony or reception is not outside where the gown will drag in the dirt. If the gown does touch the floor, you will have to be very careful not to catch your shoe in the hem. The entire dress should hang gracefully and move with you.

When making your final decision and before purchasing the gown, make certain that you receive exact prices for the gown, all shipping charges, all alteration fees, and all fitting fees. (The first fitting is usually included in the price of the dress, but second and third fittings may require an additional charge.) Add in charges for all accessories that you have selected. Total all costs before you actually make a payment so that you are certain to stay completely within your budget.

You will most certainly be asked to place a deposit on the attire and accessories that you have selected or ordered. Discuss payment arrangements with the person in charge of the gown. Do not hesitate to ask for exact dates for arrival and/or completion, for alterations and for final delivery. You may wish to have your gown stored at the shop until the time of your wedding portrait or the day before the ceremony. Ask what penalties are imposed if you cancel the order before the dress arrives or is completed. Obtain a receipt or contract where all of the above information is clearly stated so that there will be no confusion or misunderstandings. Put all deposits and payments on your credit card, protecting yourself by special consumer protection laws should the details arranged for in the contract not be followed exactly. One to two weeks after you have placed your order, call the bridal shop for a confirmed arrival date of your dress. The shop should receive this information when they place their order. About ten days to two weeks before the dress is to be delivered, call the shop to make certain that there have been no unforeseen delays.

Having Your Gown Handmade

The resources used for finding a reputable bridal salon may be used for locating a competent seamstress as well. In addition to those listed on pages 44–46 you may inquire at your local finer-fabric stores; they will often-times have the names of women in the area who sew professionally. You will also want to use the same timetable that you used for ordering a designer gown from a bridal salon. The seamstress you select may have other gowns to complete, and the time required to do the finishing work on your gown may be longer than you think. You also need to leave ample time for alterations.

After you have selected three seamstresses, schedule an interview with each one and leave an hour to discuss your gown and other pertinent information. You will want to discuss types of fabric, the amount of decoration you desire, and the amount of designing the seamstress will have to do herself. You will want to ask for references and be certain to take the time to follow up with each reference given. See if they were happy with the relationship and the workmanship that was completed.

Ask to see other garments the seamstress has completed. Check to see how the seams are finished, how the hems are sewn, and how the added decorations are attached. Are the beads sewn by hand or glued on? Is the stitching that attaches the lace invisible or can you see it?

Ask for a definite price to complete the gown and inquire as to how you will be charged for alterations or changes. Ask about her cancellation policy and the schedule and method for deposit and final payment. Will she allow you to put the amount on a credit card or does she require cash?

Here too you will want to be certain to find a picture of a wedding gown that you want to have duplicated. If you cannot find the wedding gown you desire in a bridal magazine, perhaps you can find one in a bridal salon. In this instance, you will want to see if the salesperson will let you take a picture of the gown to show your seamstress. Depending on the salon and the salesperson, you may not want to indicate that you are using the picture to have a gown made but rather as a reference to help you decide on which gown you may purchase. A picture for the seamstress is important in that it helps her "see" what you want. Oftentimes if you try to explain only in words exactly what you want, the listener may have an entirely different picture of the gown in her mind than the one you have in yours.

You will want to select one pattern to give the seamstress to make your gown. Or, if necessary, and if she is as experienced as she should be for such an undertaking, you can purchase several patterns and have her combine the different parts to make the gown you prefer. She may use the sleeves of one pattern, the bodice of another, and the train on yet another.

A considerable amount of time and money will be saved if the seamstress first makes the bodice and the sleeves out of muslin and then fits this to you. These sections are the most difficult to obtain a perfect fit on any gown, and if any alterations can first be made on muslin it will save the more expensive material you have selected for your gown.

Do not forget to sign a contract with the seamstress stating all dates, amounts, and additional fees for alterations and changes, her cancellation policy, and so on. You will need to have every aspect of your agreement stated clearly in the contract so that there will be no misunderstandings between the two of you.

Brides in Unique Situations

That which is loved is always beautiful.

Norwegian Proverb

The Pregnant Bride

If you experience the special circumstances of being a pregnant bride in today's society, it has become acceptable for you to choose to wear a more traditional style wedding gown. Some bridal salons, even though they do not advertise it, do indeed carry gowns for pregnant brides. You need to be certain, however, that you are fitted for your gown close enough to the wedding date that the measurements do not change.

The Second Marriage

As the bride, what you choose to wear at your second marriage depends on you, your groom, your age, and any special circumstances. Traditionally, brides embarking on a second marriage would wear a more "informal" gown or one that is a cream or pastel color. However, so many extenuating circumstances are involved as a direct result of today's lifestyles that you must choose what is best for you. If you did not have a large church wedding the first time and feel comfortable in a formal white wedding gown, then that is what you should have.

Keep thou thy dreams—the tissue of all wings
Is woven first of them; from dreams are made
The precious and imperishable things,
Whose loveliness lives on, and does not fade.

—*Virna Sheard*

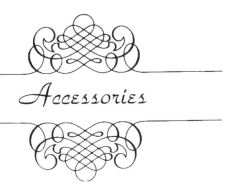

Accessories

*Y*our bridal ensemble is not complete without the accessories. Be certain to have the gown with you whenever you purchase additional pieces. Make certain the accessories are the same style, color, and quality as the gown.

Choosing Your Headpiece

The style and ornamentation of your headpiece should match the gown. You do not want a long veil with a short dress or diamonds on your headpiece if there are seed pearls on your gown. It is highly recommended that you wear your hair the way you will be wearing it on your wedding day when you try on headpieces. Your final selection should be tried on with the gown to assure that they look together the way you want them to. Practice turning and bending while you are wearing the headpiece, because some designs are difficult to make secure or to move freely in and you want to be comfortable during the ceremony and reception.

Headpieces, of course, can be anything from a circlet of fresh flowers to a magnificent cathedral-length veil. Most brides choose a veil of some sort because it makes them "feel like they are as pretty as the pictures in the storybooks."

The wedding veil, one of the most ancient of wedding customs, traditionally stood for youth and virginity, but every era in history has had a style or tradition of its own. In Far Eastern countries, it was believed that evil spirits were especially attracted to women, so, as a protection from harm, all women always wore veils. The Romans believed almost the same: that demon spirits were jealous of peoples' happiness and, because weddings are joyful events, it was necessary to confuse the demons. It was for this reason that the brides wore bright red veils; the color red, representing fire, would confuse and ward off the demons.

In European countries, the tradition of the veil was brought home by returning Crusaders. After that, the veil quickly evolved into a wedding tradition. In those ancient days, the bride was bargained for through her father and was covered in a bridal veil on her wedding day so that she was not revealed to her mate until after the ceremony.

Nellie Custis was the first recorded American woman to wear a long, white veil of lace when she married Lawrence Lewis, an aide to George Washington. Historical accounts say that Nellie chose lace because the Major had once glimpsed her face through the lace curtains of an open window—and from that day on could not stop telling her how truly beautiful she had looked!

Most books on etiquette state that mature brides do not wear a veil, even for their first marriage, and that it is generally unacceptable for widows or divorcees to wear a veil. If you are a traditionalist, you will want to follow the dictates of tradition but, if not, you may do or wear whatever feels right for you.

The majority of headpieces have two principal parts. A cap piece or hat and the veil. The cap may be covered simply with silk or satin or may be heavily adorned with beads or flowers. The veil may be made from Russian veiling, a widely-spaced weave with diamond-shaped holes usually made of a heavier thread, or illusion veiling, which is a tighter weave of nylon or silk tulle. The quality of illusion is increased by the content of silk and the tiny holes.

The style of the bridal gown dictates some-what the style and length of your veil. You may choose a style that is multilayered or you may prefer a single-layer veil. Your veil may be detachable so that you can wear it during the ceremony and take it off for the reception, perhaps leaving on the cap. Traditionally, the longer the veil, the more formal and traditional the gown. Listed on the next page are the types of veils you may consider.

Veils

Blusher—a loose veil worn forward over the face or back over the headpiece, which is often attached to a longer, three-tiered veil.

Fly-Away—a veil of multilayers that brushes the shoulder, and is usually worn with an informal, ankle-length dress or a dress with the detail in the back that you do not want to hide.

Birdcage—a veil which falls just below the chin, is gently shirred at the sides, and is usually attached to a hat.

Fingertip—a veil which gracefully touches the fingertips.

Ballet (or Waltz)—a veil which falls to the ankles.

Chapel—a veil which cascades about $2^{1}/_{3}$ yards from the headpiece.

Cathedral—a veil which cascades about $3^{1}/_{2}$ yards from the headpiece and is usually worn with a cathedral train.

For all brides, the term headpiece can be applied to a large number of bridal headcoverings—anything from a lace mantilla to flower garlands to decorated garden straw hats. Head-pieces have evolved over the centuries. The Romans chose swaths of brilliant yellow to "shield the downcast looks of virgin modesty." The Viking queens chose metal skullcaps, while Japanese brides chose and still choose the traditional *tsuno-kakushi*, a white hood that supposedly hides the horns of jealousy. The popular custom of wearing a wreath of orange blossoms, which symbolized fertility, was introduced in Europe, again by the Crusaders.

Today, the symbolic wedding crown can vary from a simple one of flowers to the elaborate headdress that traditional Japanese brides wear, which are so heavy the bride may need to be aided as she moves down the aisle to her groom's side.

To be without some of the things you want is an indispensable part of happiness.

—*Bertrand Russell*

What will look best on you? A veil, a garden hat or something more contemporary? The only way to know is to use the same process you used to select your dress. Look through bridal magazines, and visit several stores to inspect their inventory and try them on. When you have decided on a basic style and eliminated all other possibilities, you should narrow your choices down to three selections and then try on the finalists with your gown.

Wear your hair exactly as you intend to wear it on your wedding day. If your hair is smooth and pulled back, a small, exquisitely ornamented headpiece will look best. A chignon can be accented with a profile comb or pillbox. Hair with volume or thick curls can be tamed with a snood of netting decorated with some type of special adornments. Short hair is often best with a Juliet cap or floral wreath. A lace mantilla or tiara will complement any hair length.

You should also be aware of your face type. Generally, the wide brim and low crown of a garden wedding hat will abbreviate an elongated face. If your face is rounder, you can lengthen it with a high tiara or pillbox hat. If you do not know what face type you have, your hairdresser will help you understand the shape of your face and which hairstyle and headpiece will be best for you.

The following glossary may be of some help in defining the different styles of headpieces.

Headpieces

Bow—loops of ribbon or fabric worn at the crown of the head or the nape of the neck; may include ribbon or tulle streamers.

Chignon (Banana Clip)—a cluster of fabric, lace, silk flowers or pearl sprays worn at the back of the head. The ornamentation is secured on a comb or curved hair ornament with a spring-action grip to hold a large section of hair.

Crown—a traditional ornamented half-circle set toward the front of the head.

Fabric-Covered Ponytail Band—circle of elastic encased in gathered decorative fabric, such as satin or brocade; may also be adorned with beads, sequins, or other ornamentation to match the bridal gown.

Floral Wreath—a circlet of fresh, silk, or porcelain flowers that can nestle on top of the head or at mid-forehead. May also be adorned with ribbon or tulle streamers. A *forehead band,* which is a strip of decorated fabric, may also be worn in this manner.

Garden Hat—a larger, round-crown, wide-brimmed, face-framing hat that is usually made of lace, satin, straw, or other stiff, light-weight material. The brim is often boned to hold its shape and may also be decorated with ribbons and fresh or silk flowers. This hat should be worn straight across the head and low over the brow. (Remember that a large-brimmed hat will cast shadows over your face; you will want to pin back the brim for the photographs.)

Half Hat—a small hat, slightly larger than the Juliet Cap covering half or less than half of the back of the head.

Half Wreath—a decorative headpiece covering half or less than half of the head.

Headband—a wide decorative strip of stretch satin, elastic, plastic or other flexible material that is left plain or covered with more orna-mental fabrics. It is worn across the top of the head from ear to ear and may be adorned with a variety of materials.

Juliet Cap—an ornately embellished small cap that fits snugly on the top or the back of the head.

Mantilla Veils—a fine lace veiling, which gently frames the face, usually secured to an elegant comb. It may sometimes have a small cap worn underneath to add height.

Picture Hat—an embellished hat with a very large brim.

Pillbox Hat—a small, flat-topped, straight-sided round or oval brimless hat worn on top of and straight across the head.

Pouf—a small gathered puff of tulle attached to the back of the headpiece.

Profile—a cluster of fabric, lace, silk flowers, or pearl sprays that are secured on a comb and worn asymmetrically on one side of the head.

Snood—a knitted or crocheted net that encases the hair at the back of the head or nape of the neck. It may be attached to a bow, a clip, or a hat and embellished.

Tiara—an ornate crown, with or without veiling, resting high atop the head.

Tudor Hat—has a somewhat peaked crown with a narrow brim at the front, and can be worn straight across the head over the brow with the hair slightly pulled back off of the face.

Turban—a long scarf of fine linen, silk, or other fabric that is draped or preconstructed in soft folds around the head. It is often embellished with jewels.

Wreath—a circular band of fresh, silk, or porcelain flowers which are usually interwoven with ribbons, tulle, lace, or pearls. The hatpiece sits on the crown of the head.

Mantilla

Pouf

Floral Wreath

Tiara

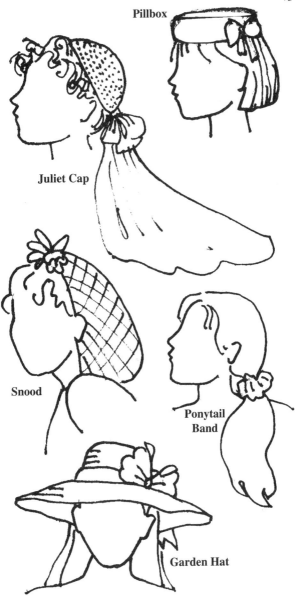

Pillbox

Juliet Cap

Snood

Ponytail Band

Garden Hat

Shoes

After your veil, the next most important item is your shoes. They should match the style and color of your gown. Pumps look nice with a long, sweeping train, while heels are more attractive with a knee-length gown. When selecting your shoes, remember to consider the ceremony and reception location. If it is to be out-of-doors on a lawn, you will not want to wear high heels that will sink into the ground or white satin shoes that will become easily stained.

Begin looking for your shoes as soon as you have selected a gown. First, it is most important that you find a pair that is comfortable. (In fact, it is best to shop for them in the afternoon when your feet are a little swollen.) Secondly, they may have to be ordered. And, last, you may want to have them dyed to match your gown or have them decorated with ornamental fabrics, jewels, bows, or rosettes. You should wear your shoes inside for a short period of time until they are broken in and the soles are scuffed; this will keep you from slipping on newly waxed or tiled floors. You will also want to wear them to the final fitting of your wedding gown to make certain your hem is the proper length.

Gloves

Gloves are usually only worn at a very formal
wedding and are optional even then, depending
on the style of your gown. They should blend
with the fabric and ornamentation of your gown
and should be coordinated with the season.
Crochet, lace, or cotton gloves are perfect for
summer, while heavier gloves are more appropriate for fall and winter. Gloves are measured
by the number of buttons. One button stops at
the wrist and would be worn with a long-sleeved
dress; those with sixteen-buttons cover the entire
arm and look best with a sleeveless gown. If you
are wearing longer gloves, you can have the ring
finger slit for easy removal at the ceremony.
You do not want to have to remove your gloves
while everyone waits.

Lingerie

Wedding lingerie serves more than one purpose:
it shapes and smooths your wedding gown and
adds its own beauty and romance to the way you
feel. This is one time you should splurge and
buy not only the undergarments that are right for
your wedding attire but those that make you feel
elegant, sexy, and pampered. Select the appropriate type of slip as well as the style of bra and
panties that best accentuate your gown. The
right petticoat can improve the shape and
movement of your wedding dress. Hoops hold
the shape of full skirts; a stiff petticoat of tulle,

organdy, taffeta, or nylon tricot works well with slightly less full skirts; and a slim sheath needs a body-clinging liner with a side slit. If your petticoat might show, be certain to choose one that is as simple or as elaborate as your gown.

The proper bra can define and emphasize your bust, if that is what you need; or it can minimize your bust if that is more appropriate with your gown. When selecting your bra, make certain that your straps will not show under your gown. If your gown is off-the-shoulder, you will need a strapless bra; if it has a very low back, you may need to have a bra built right into your dress.

You will want to buy panties that are the same color and style as your bra and in which you feel most comfortable and attractive.

You may also elect to wear deodorant pads under your dress to stop perspiration stains. If you do, make certain they are not large and bulky and that they cannot be seen under your dress.

You will want to try all undergarments on under your gown several days before the day of the wedding. You may think they will be perfect, but there is no way of knowing without actually trying them on.

You will need to buy hose that are a matching color to your gown or nude. You may believe that all whites and ivories are the same, but it is just not true. Your gown may be ivory with a cast of pink, while the stockings you thought were a perfect match have a cast of blue. Be certain you are buying the right size. Companies differ in the coloring and sizing. Once you are sure, it is best to buy three pair: one to try on while your gown is being fitted to check the size and color, one to wear on your wedding day, and one spare pair to carry with you in case you need it in an emergency.

When buying your hose, you may buy traditional silk panty hose or you may choose something a little more unique. In today's market, stockings are textured, jeweled, ribbed or made of satin. You may even want to choose a sexy garter belt for this special occasion!

Jewelry

Traditionally, many brides wear pearls with their wedding gown. However, whatever piece that has special meaning to you and accentuates the color and style of your gown is appropriate. A pearl choker may be perfect with a sweetheart or portrait neckline. A long string of pearls can be very dramatic trailing down your back with a low-backed dress. A simple locket or gold chain will beautifully complement most dresses, while a brooch or locket with a velvet neck ribbon is perfect with a Victorian or antique wedding gown. A simple bodice can be dressed up with a rhinestone pendant, or you may choose to wear no jewelry at all.

If you decide to wear earrings, you will want to choose earrings to complement your other jewelry and that are the right proportion for your headpiece and hairstyle. Drop earrings look best with a simple headpiece and upswept hair, while an ornate headpiece is complemented by simple, button-style earrings. You should ensure that your accessories do not steal the attention away from your face or your gown, that they are comfortable, and that they are in keeping with the style of the rest of your wedding attire.

To fulfil the dreams of one's youth; that is the best that can happen to a man. No worldly success can take the place of that.

—Willa Cather

Your Wedding Day Hair & Makeup

$\mathcal{M}$any brides choose to have their makeup and hair done professionally on their wedding day. Whether you choose to do it yourself or have it done professionally, you will need to "practice" several weeks before the wedding. If you want to have your hair cut or colored a certain way for the wedding, you will want to try this the first time six months before the wedding date. This will allow ample time for it to grow out or be redyed if you are unhappy with the results. Do not try something new the day of the wedding. Again, look through bridal and fashion magazines to see new styles and which styles look best with which type of dress and veil. If you use a professional for your hair and/or makeup, on the day of the ceremony you may choose to go to his or her salon or have him or her come to either your home or the ceremony site, providing there is a place for him or her to work. This is especially nice if several of your attendants want to have their makeup and hair done before the ceremony as well. Remember, too, that what you and your guests see in the form of makeup will not be what the camera sees. A professional makeup person or your photographer will be able to tell you what needs to be done so that you look good on camera but are not overly made up.

Makeup

Foundation: Use a foundation base to give uniform color to your face. Make certain that the base matches your skin color at the time of the wedding and goes with the color of your gown. During the summer months, for example, your skin may be darker than in the winter and spring. Blend the foundation from your face down to your neck and collar bone, if they are exposed. If you have dark circles under your eyes, apply a concealer to help cover any dark areas.

Blushes: Blush emphasizes cheek bones and gives your face color and vitality. Make certain the blush is also the right color for your skin tone and gown and that it is blended into the foundation.

Eyes: Use both shadows and lines to emphasize your eyes. Again color is important because your makeup should be as natural as possible. Mascara should be used on the top and bottom eyelashes and be waterproof.

Lips: Use a pencil to outline your lips and give them shape. Fill in with a small brush with creams and finish with a gloss. This will make your lipstick last longer and look professional.

Powder: Finish by *lightly* brushing a neutral matte powder over your face. This gives an even glow and helps absorb oils and perspiration.

Some general tips for makeup and hair:

1. Keep both low-key and natural looking.

2. Wear a blouse the same color as your dress while the makeup is being applied so you can make certain the color is appropriate.

3. Use matte powder to prevent any oily glare.

4. Do not have your eyes made up with dark color or outlines. They may look overly dramatic in your wedding photographs.

5. Make certain all of your makeup is water-proof. You do not want it smearing or running during the ceremony.

6. If you powder your lips before you apply your lipstick, it will stay on for a longer period of time.

7. Carry makeup with you so you can touch-up between the ceremony and reception.

Final Touches

That last finishing touch might be a lace hankie to carry with your bouquet, a Bible or prayer book that is tied with a lace ribbon and fresh flowers, a fur muff for a winter wedding, a ruffled satin parasol to top off a Victorian gown, an embroidered shawl, or a crocheted fan. Whatever you choose, do not forget the oldest of traditions which, when worn together on your wedding day, guarantees good luck: Something Old, Something New, Something Borrowed, Something Blue!

The Garter

The bride's garter is a traditional accessory that is worn just below the knee. Why? Also for luck. And, in addition to it being the "something blue" of the wedding verse, the garter serves to preserve the wedding tradition that was started in Old England. There, guests would invade the bridal chamber and steal the bride's and groom's stockings. Each guest would then take turns sitting on the edge of the couple's bed, flinging the stockings at the couple's heads. It was believed that the next to marry would be the one whose tossed stocking landed on the nose of the bride or groom. By the 14th century in France, tradition had evolved to the bride tossing the stocking, but it soon became clear that its removal was often ungraceful and embarrassing. Then only the bride's garter became the prize. Today, the groom removes the garter and tosses it, sometimes to only the eligible males. The contention is still that this ceremony indicates the next to be married.

A "bridal first-aid" kit may provide some security on your wedding day. A ripped hem, spilled hors d'oeurves or snagged panty hose are problems that can easily be taken care of if you are prepared. (This is also a nice gift to give to a bride at one of her showers. It could be presented in a decorated box to be used long after the wedding is over.)

The contents of the box should be:

Aspirin
Band-aids
Blush
Breath mints or mouthwash
Baby powder
Cleaning fluids (one solution for water-soluble
and one for greasy stains)
Comb and brush
Spare contact lens and lens fluid
Hair pins
Hair spray
Hand towelettes
Lipstick and lip gloss
Mascara
Nail file and polish
Needle and thread
Panty hose
Pocket mirror
Powder
Safety pins
Scissors
Scotch tape
Tampons
Tissues

Preserving Your Wedding Gown

*Y*our wedding gown is among the most memorable symbols of the happiest day of your life and you will probably want to preserve it. Someday you and your husband may choose to reaffirm your vows or a daughter or granddaughter may wish to wear it. In any case, you will want it to be perfect. If preserved correctly, your gown can be as beautiful for years to come as it was on your wedding day.

During the festivities, if something happens you may choose to take care of the problem immediately. For water-soluble stains, which include champagne, wine, perspiration, and beverages, you will clean with a water-based solution of water and vinegar or water and detergent. Put a towel under the fabric and blot with a damp cloth. For wine stains, rub damp salt on the spot. Allow to dry and then scrape away. For greasy stains, which include lipstick, perfume, salad dressing, chocolate and frosting, just to name a few, you will want to spot-clean with a dry cleaning solvent or spray spot remover. Hair spray also works well. Place the garment right side down on paper towels, and go over the stain, using the cleaning solution with a damp cloth. Work from the center to the edges. Then use soap and water to clean the solution out of the dress. Blot dry and be very careful with delicate fabrics.

Immediately after the wedding, your dress and veil should be cared for by a professional dry cleaner. Within two days after the wedding, arrange to have a member of your family or wedding party deliver your gown to a pre-selected and reputable establishment. They will need to remove any protective shields or bra inserts and point out any spills or stains on your dress that may have happened during the festivities. Even if it does not look soiled, the oils and moisture from your body will have an effect on the material. The cleaner should add nothing to the dress in the way of starch or sizing. After it is cleaned, you will need to let it air until you can no longer smell the cleaning fluid. Then stuff the sleeves and any bouffant parts with acid-free tissue paper and store in a cardboard box that is lined with muslin and tissue. Never use a wire hanger or store it in a plastic bag. Once a year, unpack your gown, air it out, and restore it.

Remove your veil from the headpiece and wash it carefully. To wash it, first baste the veil to the same type of cotton muslin used for your dress. Next, place this in 3 to 4 inches of lukewarm water in your bathtub, adding a soapless detergent. Carefully work the suds through the veil and fabric without rubbing, wringing, or twisting. Let the veil and backing lie in the tub, while you drain the water, and gently refill the tub with lukewarm rinse water. It will probably need to be rinsed in this manner three or more times to completely clear all of the suds. When the water is clear, empty the tub and press the veil with a white bath towel to squeeze out excess moisture. Lift the veil and muslin out of the tub, and layer on another large towel. Place a third towel on top of the veil, and gently press out additional moisture. When you have pressed out as much moisture as possible, place the veil and muslin on a dry white towel and allow to dry naturally. Do not place in sunlight. When completely dry, roll the pieces with the veil side out and cover with acid-free paper. Store in a box similar to the one used for your dress.

The poor man is not he who is without a cent, but he who is without a dream.

—Harry Kemp

BRIDAL-ATTIRE WORKSHEET

Shop #1 _____

Name _____

Address _____

Hours _____

Salesperson _____

Dress Description _____

_____

_____

_____

  Price _____

Alterations _____

  Price _____

Accessories _____

_____

_____

_____

_____

_____

Delivery Date _____

Shop #2 _____

Name _____

Address _____

Hours _____

Salesperson _____

Dress Description _____

_____

_____

_____

Price _____

Alterations _____

Price _____

Accessories _____

_____

_____

_____

_____

_____

Delivery Date _____

Shop #3 _____

Name _____

Address _____

Hours _____

Salesperson _____

Dress Description _____

_____

_____

_____

Price _____

Alterations _____

Price _____

Accessories _____

_____

_____

_____

_____

_____

Delivery Date _____

Bridal-Gown Description _____

_____

_____

_____

_____

Purchased at _____

Address _____

Telephone _____

Salesperson _____

Date Ordered _____

Fitting Dates _____

_____

_____

_____

Delivery Date _____

Dress Price _____

Other Charges _____

Total Price _____

Veil/Headpiece Description _____

_____

_____

_____

_____

Purchased at_____

Address _____

Salesperson _____

Date Ordered _____

Delivery Date _____

Price _____

Other Charges _____

_____

_____

_____

Total Price _____

Other Accessories _____

_____

_____

_____

_____

Date Purchased _____

Where _____

Alterations _____

Shoes _____

Petticoat/slip _____

Bra _____

Panties _____

Hosiery _____

Gloves _____

Earrings _____

Necklace _____

Bracelet _____

Garter _____

Other _____

_____

Index

Brides wear embroidered white aprons over their gowns, and guests discreetly tuck money into its pockets.

—*Polish Tradition*

Brides carry a handkerchief embroidered with their name. After the ceremony, it is framed and displayed until the next family bride adds her name and carries it down the aisle.

—*Belgian Tradition*

Brides wear wreaths of rosemary for wisdom, love and loyalty.

—*Czechoslovakian Tradition*

A bride once wore a golden crown during the ceremony. She was then blindfolded while unmarried women danced around her. Whomever she crowned was predicted to be the next bride.

—*Finnish Tradition*